Heart's Pilgrimage

Poems of
Michael S. O'Donnell

PublishAmerica
Baltimore

First printing

PublishAmerica has allowed this work to remain exactly as the author intended, verbatim, without editorial input.

ISBN: 1-60441-926-1
PUBLISHED BY PUBLISHAMERICA, LLLP
www.publishamerica.com
Baltimore

Printed in the United States of America

Table of Contents

The young man or woman writing today has forgotten the problems of the human heart in conflict with itself which alone can make good writing because only that is worth writing about, worth the agony and the sweat.

—William Faulkner

You have made us for yourself, and our hearts are restless until they find their rest in Thee.

—Augustine, Bishop of Hippo

Writing is like praying, because you stop all other activities, descend into silence, and listen patiently to the depths of your soul, waiting for the true words to come. When they do, you thank God because you know the words are a gift, and you write them down as honestly and clearly as you can.

—Sister Helen Prejean

BEAUTY

A Lady

There is a quiet whisper in the heavens,
 That but speaks, so low, in muted sound.
  Amidst clouds the angels nod and stare in wonder,
   For one human, this spark of Love, abounds.

  "Just a multi-tasker," rolls on a jealous taunt,
   But no—within here lies an ancient Energy
    That drives her darkness from familiar haunt.
     The Ancient of Days, her spirit has grasped,
      To bear her grace towards wounded souls,
       Offerings, through which no heart is left in want.

    Tender heart, striding veiled valleys of pain,
     Knowing sorrows: of family; of love;
      Yet known always ready to listen,
       And never, no never, to have spent her love in vain.
        Histories of lived lives may come and go,
         But your memory will leave a longing ache!
          Then the angels, well, they'll come to know…

An Attempt

Mine eyes have set on mysteries deep,
Glimpsed what awe would only dare to whisper.
O trees, the beautiful arching on your skyward arms
Has mesmerized the circling hawks!
All nature is dressing itself again for sleep.

On greens, on golds, do silently approach your goal,
There is a living fire on the hills, yet without flame!
Your fate, sealed within a call to renew,
This vibrant tapestry can seduce and rock the soul.

O reds, you greet and mingle with the browns,
Who banter and brush against your cousin's yellows.
The great hush of autumn inspires in its fatal attraction,
Through which it expires without a sound.

O painted, changing canvas, stroked with colors of splendor,
As regal as a Son, after 3 days, ascending.
Ah, to bear death's throes so magnificently,
Receiving our royal robes the day we surrender.

A Piece of Lace

Cast down this pale love,
Which has sought, too long, its own face.
Hungry eyes, pressing towards the horizon—
In the distance, approaching, that flowing piece of lace?

Shall I rescue myself or will angels protect me?
I know not what to heed.
Many the words through furtive glances,
Sown cautious is love's seed.

Care begets care, but what if unrequited?
Is love discovered in a mirror or reflected in the Image?
In recognition, completeness and desire meet;
O amidst that flowing lace, to discern her visage.

Traces of Loveliness

Day bends in its fullness
A fresh sunset falls; and
There you appear: shimmering,
Glimmering,
My rose-thorned queen—
Crimson blush,
A lilac-scented rush
Driving white streamers off
Your satin evening gown,
Tracing blues and pinks
Across a livid, dying sky—
Whose fancy a retiring sun does spy,
Leaving it aflush.
Ah, lovely barebacked beauty
Who taunts the fading light!
Twilight catches your flowing
Glowing mantle
Flinging gems upon encroaching night—
One for every sulking
Sultry heart.
Longing glance
Provokes each mind's fantasy,
Seeking a trace of hope, perchance,
Within your expanding midnight eyes.

DISCOVERY

Discovery

The present is where you are discovered—
Not to be found in past memories that haunt, nor
Future musings that unsettle—
But here, now, sustaining this creation.
Speaking, permeating presence
Residing as One foreign, yet at home in the soul.
Dawning grace, washed anew.
Here: no desire to flee, no rebuff—
The outcast, finds a hearing;
Hearing release in the heart.
Joy unending, cascading downwards,
Mingling upward into heaven.
Songs in the night that draw one into restful slumber.
Peace: flowing, rhythmic, unceasing, healing.
Deep calls to deep—
Lo, the Beloved comes…

Encounter

There is a world where whispers lie fallow,
Deception rules not the day.
Human spirits—once
Of restless pursuit,
Pressed by night's tremors and
Disheartening pasts—
Sighing, aching,
Courage coursing to the eyes
For just one long liquid gaze
Into the yearning dread of another.
Hope, in its dance,
Hangs upon the moment
That lingers towards eternity.
Here, where the Image is reflected;
Risk can no longer be deferred.
Here, amidst the silence and abetted breathe
The terror of encounter melts.
Two lives, two hearts
Once strangled by discordant years
Protected by "No",
Now beat in rhythm with time
With a surrendering" Yes".

Musing

Enter into the space, long ago, provided for you.
Here there is no sight, nor sound.
Neither smell nor touch as we know it.
(Vacant loneliness, bear me not away again.)
Here, sometimes the movement of life can lie still.
Here, in this shadowy, intuiting world,
Somewhere between light and dark
(Perchance your spirit senses this too)
A low, small cry,
A yearning rising from the foundations of the bones,
Begins its slow ascent toward the surface of feeling.
Its mounting momentum: briefly, or
For minutes, maybe several hours—
Speaks of One enjoyed.
Who enlivens like a cool crisp dawn on a fall day,
Whose softness holds the beckoning morning in silent surrender.
Whose sweetness in memory pails all else
That might preclude such musings of the heart.
"Heart of gentleness and frailness,
Break not over these words you read.
Let them warm you in your hushed moments.
From this, I will never part."

Waiting

Lord, I sense you in the winds of autumn
That puff long and warm.
Do you come to disrupt the stayed and commonplace?
Fallen leaves do limp along,
Tumbling together—
An impassioned dance in disarray.
Propelled and pummeled by an unseen Presence,
Browns and reds to slip and sway,
Eventually
Finding support to steady their stagger.
Above, the clouds that drift—
Clinging wisps of fine white cotton,
Gentle mercenaries whose
Fingers caress and rescue a pale blue sky.
I search through the streaking filaments:
Straining, can you be seen?
Is there a new Dawn amidst the day?
My heart hurtles the heavens in its silent movement;
Hope does not fade like these fine white strands,
Tempered by the winds of Time.

Waiting II

Time, its ticking, now relegated to background,
Befriended today; it passes slowly.
There is neither ache nor groan, only quiet sound—
The house, the air, scented with essence of the Holy.

No lurching thrust of prayer, no calling out,
Possessing no power to claim an audience.
No tumult of words, but wordless throughout,
A hungering awareness disclosed by acquiring patience.

There is no caricature of presence here,
No silent idol upon which raging fists pound for an answer.
Eternity awaits and surrounds, without fear,
A heart streaming upward, like a playful dancer.

Gentle Counselor, I now bear no arms.
You have stilled my soul, at Elam's rest.
Confusion has been seduced by heaven's charms,
You always woo toward that which is best.

HEALING

A Healing

Hush falls upon the green,
All eyes rivet upon this scene.
Lo comes such lovely grace,
Sunlight dances on her face.
Yellow hair and azure eyes,
To match the poppies in their sighs.

Sadness in her silence speaks,
Nature, on its tiptoes, peeks.
Their princes, while smiling, groans,
A wariness—too many unknowns.
Spring's intuition senses her pain,
By its listening, her confidence gains.

The call of green, feels just right,
To dark moods and being tight.
No pretense lies along the path,
By beauty grasped, a cleansing bath.
With eyelids closed and arching up,
Her twirling frees a soul pent-up.

Renewing is the gentle breeze,
Her spirit, lifting, does it seize.
Creation nods a healing smile,
Responding, she releases all her bile.
Holy is this sacred morn,
Mystery cradles one newly born.

The Ministry of Healing

The brokenness of being, One must repair—
Penetrating red orbs, through the pain of humanity they stare.
Liquid and dry—these tears from sallow eyes;
Hallowed hands, lifting up the timeless sighs.

The chill of inadequacy brushes across the canvas of my heart;
They come—maybe a courageous beginning, an uneasy start.
Secrets shared: bearing gifts of grief, of sorrow, of ravage,
To press back the darkness of their shadowy savage.

Scarred, bloody hands embrace the rawness of wound.
A slashing insult to pride is the risk of a burden, assumed
By the revealed Mystery of life, freely bearing past cruelty.
The "Silence of Centuries" discovered amidst such frailty.

O God of Love, required to know of suffering!
Learning to cast all anxiety under his buffering.
Ground of Being who prays in and through his people,
We place ourselves, mercifully, under this sign of our steeple.

LOVE

Corporeal Contemplation

It commences with a glance: the yearning
Playful tapping of fingertips before entwining,
Signaling the dance has begun!
Slowly, natural rhythms stir into a blending unison.
Well acquainted in knowledge and movement,
Delicate in embrace,
Spirit and body not to be broken
But to bend and turn—
Yielding reeds,
Tendered by a warm summer breeze.

The coolness of satin skin,
A lingering, unwinding, measured arching;
Sliding, biding the locking of two hearts
Into a narrowing universe.
Catapulting through shudders of delight
Into a moment of eternity,
Coursing ecstasy and forgetfulness of self.
An act of playful worship
Centuries old, crafted by design,
Committed under heaven without shame.

Now, in unspoken courage,
Allowed to be familiar with the colors of the eyes,
Gazing—no, beholding!
Beyond the painful words that blistered the heart,
Past hope, through tiresome cares—
Into the very soul.
Here, detecting the nod of God
A timeless trust echoed in touch.

Breathe, at once, that silent sigh,
Borne upon the fingertips of guardians,
Entrusted by the Divine
To offer the fragrance of all
Wordless, sacred groans,
Surrendered up through acts of giving.

Discovery II

Could sear one's soul this timeless passion,
To risk—all hearts can break after a fashion.
Love, tendered, much sought by masses,
Too often, regret, lays strewn its ashes.

Lay close, dispel; enwrap, this Sultriness of night,
Borne of God, sacred treasure, is it my right?
No more to glance askew, now knowing full disclosure,
Sweet, gentle attention, compelling in its composure.

Where spirits join, hearts are captured;
Once seared souls are now enraptured.
Should desire, too frightened and wary, flee?
Flow, echoes in the dark—through you is discovered me.

For Richard and Edna

Fifty years! Fifty years!
From whence, on this long journey, have we come?
Wasn't it only yesterday:
A boy from St. Louis and a girl from El Cerrito—
United to themselves and the Ancient-of-Days through vow and kiss?
Will yesterday's passion be tomorrow's ash?
It could never be!
For I have found myself in your eyes,
Touched upon the magic of your playfulness,
Whispered secrets in your ear for thousands of nights—
Worshiping our God through the revelation of the hiddenness in each
    other.
Our bodies have borne the fruit of three strong men and three gracious
    women,
Sturdy olive shoots around our table.
You are my beloved and I am yours.
Th Image of our God made complete when we became one.

Someday I will entrust you into eternity,
Amidst thankful tears, returning my most precious treasure.
And we will wait, wait for one another,
Where love will taste the full disclosure of Christ,
Forever embracing each other in perfect peace and
Knowledge of a love that has withstood…

To another fifty years—so be it!

Love

Winter has encircled the greying azure overhead with its cold, silvered noose,

Only to deposit an icy grip around nature—the tightening, reining in upon vitality has begun!

These days are favorable; reflective, fireplace days: where melancholic memories stroll, dreams are seductively soft and hope burns bright amidst stark beauty.

A luscious, languid day of serene, elated remembrance of my winning lady.

She is my beloved and cross; I am hers. Not through a negative rendering, but a pattern of Severe Mercy, by and through which our kind Lord has established us before one another with one command,

"Love each other and I will be able to fill you with Peace."

We are clay; being refashioned upon the wheel of daily life. We are like rough-hewn golden nuggets that must be fired in the crucible of relationship to dwell in purity.

Here is where we are appointed to co-live: caring, striving, crying, being broken, regarding, caressing and aching.

New life must contend to produce fruit. Our union is to be one of availableness, wonder, acceptance, remorse, reconciliation, playfulness, enchantment, deprivation and security.

We enjoin as separate ones, who are weary and heavy laidened, to lie within the arms of each other's forgiveness.   The awakening to forgiveness and surrendering to receive bears a great emotional and spiritual price.

God blends us in His love.

If we listen to/for Him, we will be ok; no, we will be espoused in Peace and border on ecstasy.

Christmas 2000

The Spawning

Love, unconditional, has spawned its seed,
A great hush upon the hum of the world occurred.
Eye had not seen nor ear had heard,
The Word, once spoken, has become deed.

Love, draws close, a convicting seed,
Hands to shield the eyes, disclosing regrets.
Now, too few hands to cover the leeching of secrets,
The Word, a Sword, laying bare the greed.

Love, draws close, a fallow seed,
Preparation for renewal, biding welcome, 'tis the Son!
Discovering our humanity mirrored in the Human One,
The Word addresses the weary, proclaiming, "Freed!"

If I were asked, how a god should be,
I'd desire it present to you and me.
Foolish to reason, my god would be,
Forever present, Emmanuel, in you and me.

This Fragile Mystery

Love, this fragile mystery to life,
Tell me—are you ever truly pure?
Frailty and anxiety bear such a rasping purr,
The truth behind one's motives, never to be sure.

Can one ever sound the secrets of the heart?
We are would-be gods with mortal chests!
Each morn, an earnest vow,
Intending a new start;
Returns, as sulking night,
Uncoiling its laughter.
O pride, my "purity" to smart.

Were I to cast Eros' greed upon the burning pall,
To receive my fired wound—
Healing love must play its part.
Then shower the mortal heart with diadems of grace,
Washed and bathed in purity,
One's perfection is His art.

When Downward Turns a Wayward Sky

When downward turns a wayward sky,
Wet kisses brushed upon earth's canvas,
Slides darkness foreclosing all that had been light—
'Tis when my thoughts enwrap you with my sigh.

O bright mornings, cool, too brief,
We'd gaze and touch with tender eyes,
Unlike two minnows, not fast nor fleeting,
Naked, trembling upon heaven's reef.

Alas, love's labors turned to pain,
Closeness claimed its price, left cautiously retreating;
Fear, unmasking visions of ourselves—
The illusion of the moment spoke a bitter refrain.

O let us return to days of wonder,
Where love speaks not in lies.
Through impassioned dance we fall, consumed.
Long, loving eyes have torn our fears asunder.

MEMORIES

Flight from California

Grey dawn, now greeting greying dusk,
Unending day, lingering without a rush.
Cool is the remembrance in this autumn's hush,
New beginning—are you not a gasp in wonder?
Why have you to change, tearing old roots asunder?
O heart, nudge gently these memories that banter about past haunts,
Back away slowly, so slowly, lest smoking heart should resurrect its taunts:
Of like-minds embracing,
Of arms enfolding, flowing
Liquid words, streaming softly and bantered back,
Knowing no deceiving.
Souls that touched upon some ragged edge and blended thus,
Believing.
Distanced now by miles and time,
Forever beating,
Draws wounded hearts towards nighing hope,
Forever meeting.

In Memory of Sheldon Vanauken
(A Severe Mercy)

What greying hope the indifferent have.
All too brief their tempered days are cast.
Perceived mere dots, far flung, upon some distant galaxy,
For their persistent ache, found no healing salve.

Then, lo, arrives the night, miscreant of pleasures' wrackful,
To burn in lust, consumed by evening's fever.
Slowly to greet a dawn amidst numbing arousal,
While conscience, gagged, is grasped with added shackle.

Was man meant to die, expended upon such lecherous treasure?
To negate a God who silently regards, yet weeps?
Shrill the cry, "Too fleeting," this march of time,
For thus man lives—it is his dross and measure.

But if "by chance" a night is shared,
'Tween you and I our God will forever dwell.
For Spirit sighs, in threesome, through our love,
Sailing through eyes that dare reveal, so bared.

O Davy, O Saints, I am, but not alone.
Debra, my sweet, sacred gift that stirs my heart,
To quell the pounding pulse of solitary beat,
Where fear and surrender meet and kiss within their groan.

Encompassed and seized by love so vernal,
Severe the Mercy that preceded me to your arms.
By ring and inviolate vow, God graced us a second chance,
As we gaze in wonder 'midst whispers of the eternal.

Remembrances

When warmed beside the embered fire sat you and I,
Dreaming upon the lifting notes of our nightingale:
Far off places of imagination hold heart's fast—
On schooners of splendor
Among evening's emeralds, we sail—
In love.
To sift through memories past
Discovering hidden gems and moments shared.
Secluded.
Former throes, muted by time,
Our love uprooted.
Walks along cool, white strands,
There—to sit and gaze at foam so free,
Extensions of glaucous curls
Forever kissing the land.
A scene softly beckoning you and me.
Wonderful hours of whispered wishes—
Quiet intervals, which kept no secrets,
Captured amidst the lulling, luscious blades of summer grasses.
Sun drenched,
Wind swept, leaving no regrets.
Expressions as poetic forms,
Dancing, circling higher,
Together. Lips painting picture words,
Pronounced and pondered,
Dabbling with the writ of ageless desires, and
A fire, before which
Our mellowing hearts have never wandered.

NIGHT

Another Day

Another day cranks down toward dusk.
No bids today; my spirit sags.
The mind meanders over this day's energies spent on dreams.
Sheltered in Love, I can, I must continue.

Warmed through the operation of prayer and Presence,
I make my way to evening.
The stealth of nightfall catches me not unaware;
Its steady stream is welcomed like a seasoned lover,
Whose knowledge of me induces security and
Gentle footsteps arouse passion.

Strange, these haunts of eventide,
Where peace will slip in among the silent noise
And find her home.

Day into Night

The day is shorter now—
Still, hours of long, lively drifts,
Crinkling blades of browns and yellows
Cast off, wind swept
Laid and layered out—
Along Old Stoney wall,
Demarking retreating path—
Through which a pair
Of prodding feet pass…
The day is shorter now.

Can one trust the twilight—
Those in between moments
Of luminescence upon a lingering sky,
As darkness slides within
Her muting colors—
Will she deceive or reveal bare
Those dreams, cautiously retreating
Before the advance of aging years…
Can one trust the twilight?

Behold, bold moon—
Moaning silently, seductively,
Embracing the look
Of liquid lovers, whose silhouettes
Leave such long shadows
Among the leaves…
'Tis a bounteous, bold moon.

The night is longer now—
Evening of soft-white layered tufts and
Floating filaments of fine-stretched cotton
Coursing a charcoal black-blue backdrop,
Burgeoning with far off "little lights."
To stroll, hand in hand, my crimson queen…
The night is longer now.
[10/07]

Longing

I have longed to spend this night with you, Lord,
Desiring the tranquility of your peace;
Your Presence.
Surround and bathe me in your light.
My heart to be found within your sight—
Known each path
Leading to a weeping crevice.
Here disclose a treasured secret
Harbored for months; years—reclusive demons
Shunning the Light.
Darling of my soul,
Breathe across its spirit, make it whole.
Hold heart and mind within your cupping hands.
My body—warmed to your Spirit's fire.
O constant joy of my sacred desire...

Markings

Sounds of night drift through the baffled breeze,
Small pilgrims of the twilight,
Colliding in cascading voices,
Unaware—the stalking coolness as evening approaches,
Winter's white, too soon,
Removing nature's choices.

Words of night, uncovered by the cloak of day,
Sultry symphony drips like honey,
Smoothing out discontent.
Longing, that silent seer of hearts
That know the night;
Lo, layered streams of content
Curl 'round the fireside's scent.

O night, dark temptress of beckoning beauty,
O luscious flowing drape of balm—entrance!
Sheer, soft silhouette to bathe the burgeoning senses,
Dreams cast—one star for every wishful glance.
Heart aflame, hope rising with each slinging sigh;
Do you notice,
The mark of the Divine, by chance?

PLACES

Healing Waters (of Pyramid Lake)

O raucous, ragged May!
My fears & discontent have borne
The shadows of your torrid days;
Born, the disquiet knowledge
That pretense once held at bay.
"All flesh is grass,"
Quite humbling, one would say.
Perchance I thought I'd play a god,
And what!
Escape the reaping of Time?
Grace me, lovely Pyramid,
Your merciful moments.
Do receive now my silent sighs
Upon your peaceful shore,
Flinging fears to rest
As veil of night descends.

Lovely Lady,
Such healing, reviving waters.
Behold! Each subtle surprise!
Blue heavens, bending,
To brush her kiss
Upon sweet glimmering waters.
Twilight's finger,
In shimmering mystery,
Carving a glistening silver path—
Glittering sunshine beams
Sparkle over languishing liquid;
Lulled, caressed,
Through each returning fisherman's stroke—
Swirling pools of thought,
A past disturbed,
Coming to rest
As veil of night descends.

Forlorn loon,
A longing, lonely cry
Hauntingly traverses
The surface of this azure depth;
In response, greeted by reverberating
Echoes off rocky shoulders
That surround and secure her home.
Frantic bat, spasmodically
Wings and darts
Through tepid mist,
Sliding amidst the graying structures
That daylight is abandoning.
Calling life to rest
As veil of night descends.

Not forgotten,
You adirondack chairs,
Staring out into the silence
Of drawing night;
Respectfully arranged
For "proper" distance.
If you could but disclose your secrets,
Revealing the hearts
Of those silent souls
Who have found respite
Within your wooden arms.
What dreams,
What sighs and groanings
Have ascended from your upturned,
Painted palms—
Do they ache for human arms?
Now, find rest
As veil of night descends.

And I,
As veil of night descends,
Cast cares upon cool
Streams of air
That jostle the fresh greens
Of my guardian birch tree—
Strong sinews of harmonic purity
That reach upward,
Responding to the playfulness
Of heaven's kiss.
I, learning to be at-one(-ment),
Yet aware through gift of reason.
My Beloved invites me
Into His 7th day!
Faith & hope open
To embrace my weary soul,
Finding rest
As veil of night descends…
[6/06]

Off to College

Of the echoes, well, there's silence now,
The only "thing" to greet.
Memories fill the space between walls
Where a time and season meet—
Their friendship not to be delayed.

Old walls could tell their stories!
Such dreams and laughter,
Amidst haunts and hallows
Now arise this new "ever-after"—
Grief not to be waylaid.

All life moves to groan as it transforms,
Is one to lie still or embrace?
Love, that chief among all virtues,
Does still rejoice without a face.
Its courage, should never be delayed.

Sons—strong youthful cedars,
The fruit of one's aging body—
God's gifts from once youthful passion—
Adventuresome, resilient, haughty
Arrows in flight not to be waylaid.

We, in the nest, do not rage, but
Prayerfully sigh out hopes and dreams.
Nothing, no nothing, could ever tear you
From heart's grasp, it seems.
Love, never delayed, will always waylay.

[8/07]

Weekend on the Eastern Shore

Low, this eerie, iridescent pall upon Tred Avon,
Captures time within the mystery of a momentary pause.
Red-pink streaking sunset
Bathes the yawning evening, where
Rows of scalloped, white-puffed mercenaries
Do battle, then retreat
Against the advancing Sentinel of night.
Adirondak chairs, respectfully arranged to honor "space",
Gaze out upon those silken, sullen waters,
Undisclosing tales
   Of silent sighs
      Of former watchers
         Of that shimmering, brackish bay.
Here the dreams of wishers and secret's loved
Pressed hard upon the conscience,
Flinging emboldened words and
Heaving hearts, through emotional fists,
To pound upon the grates of heaven—
O for the granted Gift of just one empathic tear!

Yet, melting sky, tantalizing in its beauty,
Does woo wonder from depression,
Raising awe upwards into a yearning ache—
Only a *fool* would not entertain this magical glimpse of heaven
And retire: knowing that he understood one moment,
But comprehended not at all.
(8/14/04)

QUESTIONS

A Question of Perspective

Is it well with my soul?
Today, I encountered the keening wail of some stilted life,
Whose ragged edge pressed hard upon the fringes of faith and hope.
Is it well with my soul? With any?

Best not to dwell on futile days or
Mischievous filled nights emptying out of a hollowed core,
That embraced the silence of the fear with cold shudder—
As touching upon some shabby-grey, grave-stoned heart.

Is peace too fragile; love a grasping, clasping moan?
Are love and hate to be balanced so precariously,
Paradoxically, upon the merest gossamer thread,
With God a sardonic puppeteer?

Faith, baptism have bound me to crucifixion (to ministry),
No longer sliding nonchalantly amidst life's ebbs and flows.
There must be a song in the night to be found!
Even, rhythmic, cascading into streams of living joy.
In the moment: a thought, a light is perceived;
If I would but learn to listen…
It could be well with my soul.

A Revisit: John 20:19-22

Too quaint are the sensibilities of man.
He loves viciously:
Grasping—the vulnerability of a crying child, in quandary; or
Misleading the gnawing love-hunger in a lifelong companion.
Paradoxical rhythms:
Shallow as a teardrop, or
Apprehended in mystery;
Complacent, yet restless;
Confident, and terrified;
Brooding, yet energetic;
Resourceful, and hoarding.
Who are we?
Estrang-ers?
Shaking the clenched fist at heaven,
Demanding our freedom without guilt!
To soothe—the quiet, desperate ache upon the bed.
To cease—the pounding temple.
To release—the ragged, hardened knot.
Approach, O sardonic night—
Sordid lover, who intuits each secret;
Preying upon our longed-for stillness.
Left, to fitfully
Roll upon the turbulence of some nearby ticking clock,
Greeting dawn through "Murine" eyes.

My, how tense we are today!
Might it not be time for *metania* (change)?

Compassion

In my hiddenness from you,
Have I learned to weep for you?
In my fear of your eyes,
Have I heard the sighs of your soul?
In the preoccupation with my tempest,
Have I shouldered your grief?
In my restlessness at night,
Have I carried your heart to God?
In the clenching of my jaws,
Have I found peace in the holding of you hand?

Compassion: "to suffer with.",
To entertain the shadows of another.
To walk with; companion.
Sometimes, to press upwards into the healing Light.
Your body, your being,
The Sacrament of Presence to me.

How Shall I Be Found?

When evening beckons and the day has been long,
How shall I be found?
Protracted is the light, lest twilight, in its stealth,
Seal us into our lonely windowed-wood boxes to uneasily await
   tomorrow.
Here, soiled souls wail for day's break,
Since dusk lays raw the wounded conscience of us all, and
Rocks through another restless, roving night.

Cannot the Spirit retire to that for which it was released?

God streams His Stillness, but
O how we attempt to purchase it with supplicated bargaining,
While Quiet waits to quiet the hollowed, heaving core.

False love is fraught with tireless games,
Demanding, weary souls bicker and ruminate,
Tasting tasteless emotions of self-induced hurt and bruising.
"Seek and you shall find," goes forth;
"Open and I will devour," responds.
Justice is weighted, mercy is turned inward, and humility,
Grossly misunderstood, seeks its revenge.

The struggle of conscience,
Attempting to right a sinking soul;
Terrible, fiercesome are the days of Love's discipline—
A hardening of the heart.

Is My Love Not Enough?

Low, the stagnant moan arises from four corners,
Yet not heard by common man!
(We have not learned compassion.)
Its crescendo peaks and verticalizes,
Sweeping upwards from the bowels of earth
Towards heaven's throne.
Foolish beggars, buying their release—
"But at what cost?" they hesitatingly inquire.
Is my love not enough?

I listen to your cry, O man,
Centuries' old retorts.
Still kick against the goads, my friends?
How you drag your weary lives before me,
To soothe the self-induced bruising of your souls.
Is my love not enough?

Ah, the appetites!
Too greedily worship those favors,
Once arrayed as glimmering gifts,
That now consume your spirit,
Chaining your will to these unforgiving gods.
Is my love not enough?

"Let us sin so that grace may abound!"
Lips that confess
While the heart trembles, adrift.
You who quietly weep in desperation
Where Standards are relativized to today's fashionable desire.
Is my love not enough?

Idolized play-toys guarded by anxiety—away with you!
Grasp the plow without the backward glance.
Purity—she beckons and woos her takers,
Such soft and muted charm!
My grace is free and costs you everything.
Is my love not enough?

Life and Death

Life and death,
Poised
On slender thread,
A balance:
One regards renewal;
The other a tragic tale.
But for us humans,
Do they not compliment each other?
For out of death spills life—
We know it in our nature;
'Tis the way of all nature.
Winter's frigid hand
Must kill
Before she can make alive.
Is this not the way of grace?
From out of nothing—
The impossible—
Does not God make anew?
From the rib that covers anguish;
Before the knife can ever fall;
Out of the womb, so still and barren;
Off rough-hewn wood and empty tomb.
Out of stupor we strain to listen
Peer out amidst horizon's shroud.
A still small voice,
It call and lingers,
And bids, "I've opened heaven's door".

Quest

How does one capture inner expressions of faith with words?
So often words are useless, meaningless,
Vain attempts to appease guilt and inadequacy,
Excess baggage to be cast aside—
They do lead me from your presence!
Rhythm of my heart, be my prayer;
My life's pulse to adore You!

Too many lives cascade and slide from one conflict to another;
Where lies our Rock?
Are agonies required to bear us boldly before your face,
That the soul's eyes might truly apprehend?
Is the 'splendor' of life found within this "grass" that withers, or
Is it borne upon the Breathe from Ancient of Days?
You heal, but then, You heal not.
Saints nurtured through suffering: your gift
To cleanse, to save,
To lance the wound of pride and
Hang humility within a war-torn soul.

O night that sardonically grins,
Ever pressing upon the distress of the lonely,
Who groan and sense no break of night—
Can there be no rest between your sighs?
O night, oh time for song—to dance
Upon the strings of quiet joy;
The knowledge of the Crucified,
Where hope takes on a most resplendent charm,
Enwrapping the infinite in the present moment.
There, to linger, lovingly linger
Upon the soothing Silence of His eminent call.

What is your treasure, o man?
It lies in your coveting.
Not of experience that can be touched or observed,
But of interior chambers draped in secret shrouds,
The cause of loneliness masked upon a million faces,
To whom the night reveals only the shadows of their existence.
How precious are these lives to Him!
He surely will cast off those shabby graves-clothes,
Bathing the night in living Light.
Alleluia! What a God to know.
[1983]

What Is Forever?

Forever strains before a distant horizon.
A struggle for a vision that resembles but haze.
Bygone days,
Streaming red sunsets—
We'd clasp "forever" within our gaze.

Warm smile captured in memory, unending,
Purring heart sifts melancholic pain.
Forever sounds its stillness in the fathoms of the soul,
Where hides but One
Who knows its solitary wane.

O banish, ill-misfortune.
The Ancient-of-Days advances his call,
Gentler than the stealth of New England fall.
Vibrant, coursing upon the rhythms of cool, spring air.
The web of life spun within your care.
Though my heart should cry out a wayward ring,
I am forever bound to my King.

Where Have You Gone?

Where have you gone, O my Lord?
Countless hours I have searched for You;
Cool nights, timid days,
They break across my horizon—
Straining, into which I peer...
Where have you gone, O my Lord?

Where have I gone, O Lord?
Broken, gasping, ragged of soul;
Have I slain the presence of your Spirit
Rather than being slain by you?
How shall I discharge my duties as a son?
Where have I gone, O Lord?

(Pause)

Humble, contrite heart,
Swept up within the movement of Love—
In Christ, ashamed no more!
Angelic echoes, breaking forth across the horizon—
Closing my eyes as I receive...

STRUGGLE

A Modern Psalm

O Lord, my sins are ever before me.
They clash about and grate upon my soul.
Your Spirit moans within me
And the conscience that She loves to soothe now
Aches in grief with memory of quiet rest.
O Lord, I have no defense before You—my excuse runs
Dry as useless prattle.
I feel sin hang its hat and cross my threshold;
My teeth chatter at the coldness of its breathe!
Fingers, like ice, begin to tighten and constrict.
My body groans in its travail.

Yet, how alluring this terror is!
I am controlled and drawn onward by this inner force.
My will to possess this desire is almost overpowering.
My coveting rages and attempts to bind my will to its own!

Father, I have no place left to turn except to you.
Will my song in the night rise like incense once again?
The years of your love seem wasted and shunned,
I have hidden my face from you,
And yet I yearn to please you—always!

(pause)

O Grace that abounds all the more!
O Love divine that covers my sin!
O Spirit that has breathed on me!
Darkness cannot hold my soul;
I am purchased for eternity!
I tremble with release as the heaviness
Lifts from my heart...

Your love so clean, so pure, is mine forever!
My finite weakness sighs and stirs
Yet how your gentleness stills it!
Gone is the sin that screamed inside my chest—
Gone is the guilt that pierced me through as arrows!

I kneel, covered by your healing blood.
The quiver of my heart is held within the caress
Of all consuming forgiveness.

Eagerness for you and all that you are fires within me.
I come, O Lord, I come…
Grace has claimed me once again.
I am sealed.
I am secure.
I am yours, O Lord, forever.

An Ode to Words

Words, words, thousands upon thousands of wordy words,
Well-aimed and misdirected.
How to convey tender mercies from such inner raucous rancor!
O dolorous dreams that require release upon the couch!
Lips that burst with billowing boasts while eyes do glance askew—
Can they know my deceit? Can they penetrate my cover?
Are my clever words not clever?
Shall the naked flesh of my soul be laid open by the eager eyes
  of those who hunger for my guarded secrets?
Yet the thief fears too—
Their glance to steal acknowledges possessed secrets too!
Such secrets—to ache, to tremble,
To hollow out the human core.

Would not silence be our cure?
Stand brave, my friend.
O Silence, be your cure—through foolish deeds, beguiled with guilt,
Past forgotten angers, whose furious fists still pummel the heart;
Forge longings of disquiet and despair—quaint lovers of frailty,
Whose alluring arms seek to enwrap us to her bosom—
O where is the assurance of the calm of night?
O where is peace that does not deceive nor
Is shallow as a tear drop?
Do I dare to listen to my dread?
O words begone! O ego, depart!
The roll of rage must cease.
Such dread of days must slink away,
As I learn to listen.

Stillness: bear no arms against me,
Nor wage your tiresome wars.
No words of meaninglessness—

Now beckon me with muting sounds.
The cries of silence are for me!
Soft shimmerings of forgotten love,
Quietly calling, patient within the depths
To be discerned without words.
O silent Word!
My heart glides over your soothing secrets.
I am anew and cuddled like a child,
A timeless purring perceived within my flight.
Closing my eyes amidst Silence's whispers,
Knowing my God is here—
I'll draw near…

How Travels This Night

How travels this night, my friend?
Have you procured your peace at any cost?
Is your hollowed heart a caged fool,
That hums with business and knows not its loss?

Has your God smote you with his iron?
Does pride still contend for a hearing at any cost?
Can your smile still seduce and enchant,
Flung up from the abyss of a sliding soul that knows not its loss?

An even layer of dust has choked once liquid dreams,
Since streams of loneliness are sequestered at any cost.
For when the rattling sabers of night are slowly unsheathed,
They proceed to cut and expose a wounded heart that will forever know
    its loss.

O sheath, draw back your trusted companion;
Let the pilgrimage to Love begin, again, at any cost.
For feign do I deceive to not perceive this yearning,
Vain is the searching heart that knows not its loss.

[1995]

Journey

Shall paling rose regain it's vibrant color?
Does wonder lapse, with young life torn apart?
A hint of dew; oh, please, just healing touch!
Draped, mysterious—herein lies her heart.

Her body cut, immortality questioned,
Scissored hands that belie a haunting trust.
Heart that soars into an embracing Abyss,
Faith lies quiet; to be grasped, a must.

Weathered, a sacred temple yet stands,
Azure eyes, reflecting a determined measure.
Stillness—healing arms to soothe the groan,
A smile regained—her priceless treasure.

Night's Call

The night has called me to itself
Yet I find no respite.
I have run the day, yes, busied myself,
Escaped the anger & discord
That slithers just beneath my consciousness.
My pet peeves are my right, my existence!
The insults to my heart I cling to,
Tight fisted, with a stance.
My pulse pounds,
Insomnia claims another victim,
But I am cool; discrete.
I will have my day; my justice!

Funny—my song in the night rings hollow;
Still, I find no respite.

Routine

I am surrounded by the routine; the commonplace.
Burdened by the drudgeries of my past,
Fighting to escape my stifling mortality—
Where is my miracle!
Where is that salvation experience
To enwrap me
In its golden threads of painless eternity!

It is nonexistent.
Here lies the rub: eternity within the commonplace of the routine.
To still the soul within the routine; the commonplace.
Is this my miracle?
I have hidden my heart in your Word—
It breaks forth across the new horizon of the present!
The routine, the commonplace—this is my miracle!

Shelter from the Storm

(Father)
There is a world out there that presses in,
(Moments can become too cruel!)
Allowing no pretense, no veil to hide the uncertain soul.
Rent
By world news,
Aching joints,
The stalking of time.
My humanity seeking—
A shelter from the storm.

Quickly!—retreat to quiet places,
To still the uprising of an unsettled mind.
That shimmering, winging heart,
Now waylaid,
Straining into the horizon
Pausing for that once familiar echoing of "peace!"—
A shelter from the storm.

Fantasy and dreams to melt my day into chocolate,
To cope I will not cope!
Staring out through glassy, expressionless eyes,
Reality claws its way along some ragged edge—
Too close, too close!
O for some savior to befriend me—
A shelter from the storm.

Reflections cannot reveal self-knowledge
(Unless one knows how to look).
"Who are you?", a mirror asks back.
(Do you not recognize me?)
Why...a face crowned with thorns and missing tufts of beard.

(Try as I may, I cannot look away!)
With all my might, I am drawn to this fright.
Soft, warming Light
Bathes my wounds tonight.
Deep within, One enters in—
A living shelter from the storm.

The Cardinal Sin

The eyes of night do cruelly search around,
To steal our darkest secrets, and catch what can be illicitly found.
Yet eyes, for all their beauty, in myriads of sight,
Must make way for ears, as colors mute at night.

Hearing—oh how keen, as if you'd had a choice,
With what fierceness and delight—your quiver for a voice.
For a moment, just one moment, a man's confession said,
Once overheard—what glee! An appetite is fed.

Lo, the Man, so loving, smiles down upon His kind,
"My saints, my holy ones," the blameless of his find.
Soon tearful turns Love's countenance, vulnerable His breast;
Thrust deep the arrows from drawn lips,
"My people hiss like all the rest…"

Too Accustomed

I have grown too accustomed to the day.
Its face, routine, bears little sway.
To catch one's breathe, no time, delay.
I have grown too accustomed to the day.

I have grown too accustomed to the evening.
Anxiety's pulse, my temple's burn, I'm weaving
A layered mask, with plastic smile, deceiving.
I have grown too accustomed to the evening.

I have grown too accustomed to the night.
No liquid dreams, my mind pressing body, tight.
Should I surrender, a heart that beats with fright!
I have grown too accustomed to the night.

O day of grace that only shudders;
O evening beckoning with muted colors;
O sardonic night, where nothing flatters;
I have grown too accustomed to what little matters.

TRUST

A Season

There is a time and space to dwell—
In stillness, a fruitful, fertile soil.
Approaching night shall cloak our sight,
Lies fallow, this once churning hell.

Through tantrums, through tears that never dried,
Some wretched creature has cried this night:
Who loves the shadows yet hates the light,
Through days of complacency, wasted in pride.

Honoring, the creature seeks its creator;
Fool—the chasm of the Abyss, too wide.
Faith bridging the distance, Hope the traveler,
Patience and courage to court at his side.

Love has watered, the soul is ready,
Transformation ensues—its course is steady.

A Turn for the Better

Alone in my consternation,
At risk for fantasy and fascination.
Awful, the false tribute paid to oneself!
Isolated, scheming soul, hidden in a shelf.

Worry's cords have wound this bundle tight,
Daytime's tremors, find their calm in night.
Refuge of retreat, speak soft and slow to sigh,
Hearts to meet, while soul, surprised, takes flight.

Now, two wills as one, unequal but complete,
Songs in the night, lifted up, replete.
Tender me, Gentle Good, a most ragged lover,
Blanket of forgiveness, guilt & nakedness, cover.
[6/06]

Doubt

Doubt; discomforting fear.
Sometimes they grip my heart like a vise;
My thoughts, to languish and stutter.
The doldrums of life—where is my enthusiasm?
Moments pieced together through anxiety;
Courage as brazen as full retreat.
If only to feel, to see, to touch,
To be grasped by your unseen presence!
Then I could believe—well, better.

"If you saw, there would be no need for faith.
I desire to win your love, wooed and freely given.
Your life compels you to seek outside yourself.
Trust in Whom I have placed inside of you.
Of your life—I am curious and patient with you.
Listen to my Word with your heart;
Reason it with your mind.
To be loved is a disciplining experience,
With calm found after the storm."

Hiddenness

Hiddenness.
    A protection? A running away?
    From what? From whom?
    To whom? To what?
Am I ashamed of myself; my cruel and abusive actions?
    Of my sin that hangs its hat too readily
    By the door of my heart?
    Do I fly
    Into the arms of that Ancient of Days
Whose knowledge of me is both profound and quieting?
    Whatever my motives,
    Allow me to stand under your presence.
As one estranged, but now found and accepted.
    Let us hide together
    In the cupped hands of the Father:
    You, my Way and Teacher;
I, your friend and sister.

Sometimes

Sometimes this nature of mine can consume me.
Reflected in sins and passions that grate upon the soul,
Forgiveness seems too cheap: a mouthed prayer,
Blessing motions in a box—*salvus* is not whole.

Days where life's gift reveals empty hands,
And the brilliance of love is like a grey tomb stone.
I cannot love out of which has not been transformed,
Its demands do ache the very marrow of the bones.

The purpose of Christ—the breaking of perceived freedom;
To consume and possess life is to lose.
In Him lies peace and, His two expectations:
Humility and repentance he will never refuse.

To Be Known

To be known! A rather frightening affair.
Having one's secrets laid bare against the will!
'Tis the stealth of Insult and Shame, two incredulous rogues
Who tear apart the veil of "respectable decency",
To cast a forsaken fellow upon the gallows of the unclean.

But—to release a secret of one's own volition!
Engaging the ear and the heart of another in intimate attention,
Airing stale chambers that now gulp freedom's scent.

Or, with chest pounding out it's warning cadence,
To trust another, of some familiarity, with a burden.
To tremble, to shudder so magnificently,
Releasing a sigh that rolls upwards of heaven's gate;
Coddled and held in the embrace of a Creator, or friend.

To be drawn—cautiously, pensively, involuntarily—out,
Aware of Love's brush against the loneliness of one's soul

Printed in the United States
108422LV00006B/395/A